Dawn Wood

Quarry

Templar Poetry

First Published 2008 by Templar Poetry

Fenelon House,
Kingsbridge Terrace
Dale Road, Matlock, Derbyshire
DE4 3NB

www.templarpoetry.co.uk

ISBN 978-1906285-08-1

Copyright © Dawn Wood 2008

Dawn Wood has asserted her right to be identified
as the author of this work in accordance
with the Copyright, Designs and Patents Act 1988.

All rights reserved. This book is sold subject to the condition
that it shall not, by way of trade or otherwise, be lent, resold, hired out
or otherwise circulated without the publisher's prior consent, in any form
of binding or cover other than that in which it is published and without
a similar condition including this condition being imposed on
the subsequent purchaser.

For permission to reprint or broadcast these poems write to
Templar Poetry

A CIP catalogue record for this book is available
from the British Library

Typeset by Pliny
Graphics by Paloma Violet
Printed and bound in Turkey

To Beth, Graham and Marianne

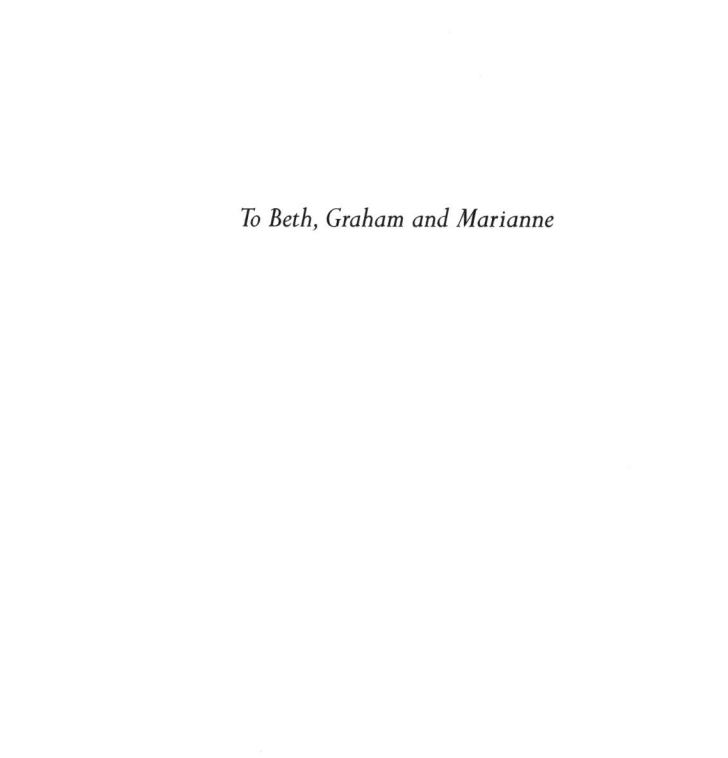

Acknowledgments

Thanks are due to the editors of the following, in which some of these poems were first published: *Cencrastus, Edinburgh Review, Magma, New Writing Scotland 19, Poetry London, PN Review, Poetry Review, Stand, Templar Anthology 2007, The Red Wheelbarrow, The Times Literary Supplement*. The concluding lines of 'Imagining a Palestinian Sunbird Drinking Lilac' are taken from the song 'Lilac Wine' by James Shelton. 'Travels of St Thomas' includes a quotation from Democritus' theory of atoms. My thanks to The Carnegie Trust for a research grant which led to some of this work. Special thanks to the many people, named and unnamed, who have given encouragement and inspiration.

Contents

I

To a Man Cast in a Hard Role	3
Nearing Midsummer, Highland Perthshire	4
The Silver Stag	5
Betrayal	6
Imagining a Palestinian Sunbird Drinking Lilac	7
Fruitless	8
Quarry	9

II

Likeness	13
I Will Give You Acupuncture	14
The Twins Weigh Out the Tomatoes	15
Greenhouse	16
Town with Meat Factory	17
Shibboleth	18
Balloon	19
Encounter	20
Gallows Hill	21
In Vivo	22
Magnificat	24
Revenge Tragedy	25
Geometric	27
The Untitled	28

III Herd Book Sonnets

Sire	31
Dam	32
On Visiting the Aberdeen-Angus Headquarters in Perth	33
Anthropomorphic	34
Rawburn Transformer	35
Arc	36
Crisis	37
Birtie	38
Doublings	39
Memorial	40
Laird	41
Apprentices	42
Canntaireacht	43
Yvonne Says You Can Pose Any Question to the Universe	44

IV

That the Attitude Influences the Result	49
Travels of Saint Thomas	50
Comparison of a Black Labrador with a Sikka Deer Skull	52
Sonnet of the Noctuoid Moth	53
The Herd Sorts Pinecones	54
Valentine	55
Wordpigs	56
Man and Atoms	58
Number, Weight and Measure	60
Cleave	61
Hybrid	62
Second Wind	64
Key	66
Galatea	67
Garden	68

> ...softly he curved
> To rest the delicate foot that is in my hand,
> Empty as a moth's discarded chrysalis.

- Kathleen Raine, The Silver Stag

I

To A Man Cast In A Hard Role

The end, when it happens, will be local,
perhaps in a year or so. Meantime,
my advice would be to sing —

sing as if you have stumbled
into a sweet, stone cathedral,
as if to lift the pigeons with you from the greasy steps;

those diamond notes could stir
the founder's marble foot,
could score a plate-glass dove through stains.

Stand on your bones, breathe with the building.
The end, when it happens,
will have you laughing —

you and the others —
biting mouth ulcers, still unable to prevent it —
then, give in.

Nearing Midsummer, Highland Perthshire

I am reminded of the man
who invented the microscope:
we are belly-down Leeuwenhoeks in the heather,
looking through our spyglasses
at these autonomous, gently moving animals —

they are in their environment, not us;
the gamekeeper scribbles the days off his calendar
knowing that time moves differently on the ridges
and we are amazed, as usual
at the unmistakable nature of the once invisible

stags, at the vigorous fronds of their antlers,
at the way the hinds arch their necks
to smell what the wind brings.
It is the pale hind that he would take out
if it was after the twentieth of October —

she is old, and her child beside her, first,
although his best day would be a switch,
that single point, as effective as a spear
and a heavy-bodied hummel.
He would never aim for a star beast: an imperial or a royal

nor would he shoot a red deer over
the Rover bonnet, spooking the others,
nor would he slaughter hundreds, to save
the newly planted alder, rowan, pine and birch
instead of raising fences.

The Silver Stag

Like Macbeth or a farce, four of us
in 'real-tree' jackets, caps down
deuking from hillock to hillock.
The deer winded us on a Westerly and bolted

towards the next estate hours since.
We scavenge golden plover ghost-whistles,
a sea-eagle spanning; I think 'bath-spider'.
The wind catches the keeper's '… *looking forward* …'

'*50 in the hollow*' radios George, from Lake Con.
We're on our stomachs. Ed and I lag,
make small-talk. I ask his sir-name.
We study droplets. Long for gun-shot. Sleet mists

the target. Finally the stag-thud. Mike's first.
And how alive he looks. His long lashes.
His male smell. His mouthful of grass.
His portioned heart. Our four-fold need.

Betrayal

As the Chieftain
buries his wife
alive in a cage
at the promontory
of the lake called Dog;

as the stag of twenty hinds
roars October's cull
on the red cairn;

as a rowan hones
a hard winter
with many prayer beads.

Imagining A Palestinian Sunbird Drinking Lilac

So much nectar
        you could swim in it
or it in you

you could assimilate
a sugar flux
spin a sun-drop into a net

conduct
        exchange
                conduct

you could   hold
                  spill
                  hum

a prayer into a wing

isn't that she
coming to me
nearly here

Fruitless

My relatives all preach.
We were sent on beach missions,
red and white uniform.
We flexed our limbs,
we had the sun on our backs.
We played Murderball,
my staved nose set itself.
A little girl at Rossnowlagh
pleaded, her Grandmother
reassured her: but sweetheart,
you're already saved.

Quarry

Indeed, there was a god, who wondered
how will I get that woman to notice me?
He was half-asleep when it came to him —
heart-shaped, he thought.

So he laid stones along her path to work;
sometimes shone the sun or glinted rain
on an especially heart-shaped one.
Occasionally she picked them up.
So many, they weighted her.
She learnt to smile, to walk on.

Hmmm, he thought, *something else* —
chewing gum, trodden into flat hearts;
bird droppings, splattered unmistakably;
the stance of a raw potato on the traffic island
where she stood to cross the road;
a heart-scrape on the paint on the radiator in her room.

She noted all these. He became more adventurous —
he arranged a heart-red remnant
of the skin of a chilli on her dinner plate;
he bobbed a tiny heart-shaped piece of cork in her wineglass.
She saw. She swallowed. And he knew he had her.

II

Likeness

The way she sits, resigned
reminds me of my family's pale-eyed
women. Her mind
will be busy as she trades the rain
for a trinket
distraction while driven.
She is always naïve and she knows it
a second too late as she sifts
through her money in front of a stranger
trying to find something appropriate;
always surprised how this gaze
is reflected, now from the fourth
generation she has known.
She forgets each one bargains
to run from the previous,
looks at her watch as her mother did —
wrist tipped,
bones too near the surface.

'I Will Give You Acupuncture'

I'd been hoping for a herb potion,
but the Chinese Doctor has left the room
and me, threaded to the machine.
These flutters of — let's face it — pain —
wheedling across the small of my back,
are taking me to all my default places, Beth:

there go those tufted horse-worms
travelling on tarmac between bog-lands,
and a mother who would even brake
the car for one, I think, but you say, more likely
we were cycling, we would jump at the chance
to return that little mossy scroll to the verge;

and there goes the squeeze of an oilcan
and our good wool coats ruined;
(was it the stiff folds from the yolk that annoyed us?
Or being dressed in the same blueness?)
We hadn't been scolded, since our weekday gabardine
that damp Monday, was still on the line;

and the march of the *Darkling Thrush* —
the only poem I know well enough
for this situation, because we revised with it,
knowing that grey climate trembled
through with bog-cotton and buoyant skies and us;
and there skips that poor caterpillar — who asked

pray, which leg comes after which?
who lay distracted in the ditch,
now she's up and running with the rest, inspired.

The Twins Weigh Out The Tomatoes

He used to bring us Cherry Bakewells.
Our job for him was to do the tomatoes.

They smelt exclusive, like greenhouses.
A pound to a brown bag — that was 4 or 5,

and a puzzle with the sizes —
to use the whole box, not one left over,

but avoiding the yellow, wet sort since
they would seep. When we were good, we would race,

a box apiece; less to spill than with flour or sugar.
He showed us how to seal the bagfuls between two twists:

whip it round too roughly and it would tear,
too gently and the top would gape;

actually the correct weight of the tomatoes
did the trick, along with a confidence in the wrist.

We would efficiently fit the bulges
back in the shallow tomato box, alert for the van.

They'll remember the quality, Bertie
when they've long since forgotten the price.

Greenhouse

That home garden had two poplars.
We would always scurry,
one Saturday, come autumn,
to rake those sweet-smelling, mottled leaves.
That pair shimmered in the weather,
growing taller.
My father fretted over his roof
and the roofs of his neighbours.
So he topped them into stunted landmarks.

On August the fifteenth,
I had been in my own allotment.
The previous tenant had left his greenhouse
top-heavy, unsafe — smelling of almost-tomatoes,
with the cob-web of a pink plastic crucifix
and a fire extinguisher.
But I'd dreamt — was it Mary,
from the plot-next-door?
A dark omen, a splintered body.

So, I borrowed a helmet from a building site,
gloves and a hammer. Spent hours,
easing panes from their frames.
I came in, tired, heard about the bomb.
Returned to my tools, to smash glass.
My lovely, home-town people.
My father would have brought you
sweet things named for places:
Paris buns, Genoa cake, Battenberg with marzipan.

Town With Meat Factory

Translated characters, above a sink, have a hint
of red-skied old Soviet optimism, but probably read,
Europeanly, *Wash Your Hands Thoroughly;
Report Any Illness.* This pie-shell making machine
is set up to dream saving for new Ukrainian bungalows.
That brick pink, semi-frozen meat,
manoeuvred in blocks to the hopper, was reared elsewhere

like these professional young couples,
hair correctly tucked in nets, fingers in gloves,
to firmly pat monotones of pastry discs.
The off-cut negative space, drifts, flour-quiet, entire,
up and back over a roller, then slightly
hypnotically lumpily, since one-width-in has become,
and is persisting to be, detached, from the metal surface.

At school we had off-cuts like this — foil sheets
of absent milk bottle tops from the Nestlé factory,
kindly hung by sixth years in the assembly hall
for the Christmas play *(The Winslow Boy, Alice
in Wonderland, The Crucible)*, or sellotaped in arches
for the Valentine's disco. That terrible, cold press:
layer upon layer of why you couldn't dare to dance.

Shibboleth

She left them a note to walk the dog
and I shouldered her luggage
while the choir who know me best
would dart looks,
fascinated by twinhood.

They would keep it up
even after the obvious —
hairstyle: maybe hers is thinner,
and the glasses she'd worn
since we were eleven

after the German measles
when she'd come out of Belfast
humming hospital radio.
It might be the single, deep breaths
that have left me taller.

She'd never heard our Mag and Nunc
and I couldn't make her see
till then, the pattern:
call — response — and call again,
or the way the composer

might play around in the setting
of his version or even let it stream,
ears of corn, through his fingers,
ringing true to self
and world without end.

Balloon
i.m. Bertie McFarland, 1924-2001

His loss —
the loss of him —
is like a red balloon
bidding with the blue
growing both intense and distant;

remember the sky over Disneyland
and the black-eared drifting mice
so many of them,
like bulletins or jokes
about cost, impermanence, joy;

remember how you couldn't lay flowers
where he didn't lie
and how Jenny's own balloon
escaped over the march
that first visit;

we always knew it would require a flight
a wandering
and happily he would have made a link
with the rowan berries
by the boundary and into the next field.

Encounter

after Czeslaw Milosz

A father tells his young daughters what a hare looks like;
of his life — how his mother learnt
to warm the corn for the slow-laying hens in winter,
of the boy and the horse he couldn't lead towards the yard,
of the appearance of a fox,
        of a hare.

They talk of how it differs,
they will know from his description.

Is it later, when they walk
around a foreign wood,
searching for the tapping, for a piebald wing?

        He's gone of course;
one daughter reads the words in wonder;
one rounds the corner of the edge of trees, in pain,
the hare is waiting.

Gallows Hill

Not that he would need to give them names
he would know them from the shapes

of their whorled foreheads — perhaps
those twin calves did influence the weather

as in the myths — certainly Walter
had just mentioned all pairs of them

when a deluge threatened to shelve
the quarry road into the newly dug lake,

to float store seeds from the grange,
like wayward children, into the green

and there was Val's laral bucket
as ever in place — not that she would need

to give them names, she would hear them
in the slate-filtered rain, sounding tin.

In Vivo

My research project was
to harvest quantities
of monkey kidney cells.

I was to shear holes
in their outer membranes
and to add hormones

extracted from frogs' eggs.
Then I was to look
for peaks of sugared protein.

The fractionator beeped
with confidence — I set
it up to dole out little

drops into epindorphs,
rotating on a carousel,
overnight.

Drip, drip, drip, the trouble
of not being able to have
a daughter.

Every time, the trace
I checked flowed low
as honey, smooth and cunning.

Every morning, my thought:
infertility.
He announced

we would punch
holes in my ovaries.
Enough was enough. I left,

and suddenly
you tagged along: a pulse
of bitter-sweetness, no harm done.

Magnificat

Y
ou
are a
drop in the
ocean. You are
a drop of ocean. You
are a drop of magnificent
ocean. The ocean is surely
magnificent in the drop-
ping of you.

Revenge Tragedy

'It locally contains, or heaven, or hell;
there's no third place in't.'
- John Webster (1580?-1634)

It took five years to clear the stage,
to leave only
pillars rising to an arch,
dark walls, running water —

the preoccupations
of drinking, hand-washing;
and a grid fitted to conduct waste
past grained floorboards.

I am frugal, I have saved
few objects — fragments of a mirror;
a book to swear on;
the sweet, delicate fruit he hands her;

curtains to facilitate scene changes
and red, always shades of red.
The floor is tilted forwards severely —
this is why the thin liquid runs —

some from each person — and glints;
although I can't predict
when each rivulet will join or branch
or land in someone else's lap.

Not that any of this is real, of course.
I'm home and lying in this bed, paying
attention to the echoes
of this October debris wrinkling

in a sky that's faintly orange.
As yet, there is no sign of sunrise.

Geometric

His wife has posted ground almond sweets,
cut on the bias, drizzled with silver.
I am offering him a Cherry Bakewell while we wait
for the kettle: *cherries for children* he almost shivers.
My daughter has been practicing diagonals,
angle to angle, she defines them,
joined with a ruler and a sharp pencil.
The full moon, he replies, is neither a man,
nor a hare, nor even a woman gathering rice,
rather, a lover might cry — *you are so beautiful,
why, even the moon has a mark.* The sweets
are soaked with icing. The moon is spherical.
The kitchen is rented. The moon cannot be blamed —
we have not seen it whole, until we have been damaged.

The Untitled

i.m. Vincent Rattray, Dundee Artist

Girl with Brush, Mother with Cards.
Barber, Sailor. Dog Ring.
Flower-eyed Boy and Set of Grippies.

Man Holding Skull, Sliced Apple, Pale Ale.
Woman in Rimmed Glasses and Feather Boa.
Couple with Visor and Harmonica.

Rush Hour People and Woman
with Multi-coloured Sad Eyes.
Broken Arm Between Dancers.

Woman, and Child with Tongue, Horse.
Woman with Bra Showing, Man, Dove.
Man Hugs Yellow, Table of Onlookers.

III The Herd Book Sonnets

Sire

These herd books make me think of Scottish
strip-the-willows — let me lead you for example
down the *Laird of Morven's* maternal side
via various *Idas*, back to *Mary of Learney;*
the sires along the way are fragile branches
barely mentioned: *The Baron, Magnet, Fortitude,
a Prince* — a note beside the Laird himself outlines
his journey West, the settling of a seed account,
when he was shot at Liverpool dock.
Indeed, the good die early, just like the pony
we used to sing about in play ceilidhs —
he's gone, where all good creatures go —
leaving an empty stall, a bridle and my Father
on his next party piece — The Yellow Rose of Texas.

Dam

Gone, as with *Eclipse of Greenmyre* — there,
appended to his great, great, great grandam
Dorrit, is a letter from the stockman's son
admitting the loss of *Eclipse* — he having
administered undiluted sheep-dip.
And gone like the *Galloways*, *Mary
of Meikle Culloch* to *Modesty* of the same —
removed after the rare, first edition of the first
Herd Book — since no animal has been allowed
of whose purity there is the slightest doubt.
With my mother, not so much a ceilidh
as a mission in her case and her choice
of song would have recommended washing
in the wonder-working blood of the lamb.

On Visiting The Aberdeen-Angus Society Headquarters In Perth

Big black squares on the boardroom walls.
Some painters seized on the undulations of the dewlap
and the brisket or met flat backs like horizons
with flocks of ducks, Queen's castles, waterfalls.
Notable animals, with names like found poems:
Blackbird, Magnolia, Reunion, and *Paris,*
the last of his line, whose stuffed head
hangs just inside the yellow door, but alive
and you would have sunk your debt-worried face
into his lived, real, warm pelt, in the year
of the short corn; you would have groomed him,
advertised him in a sea of straw,
you would have played these creatures,
blunt notes from the belly of your black pipes.

Anthropomorphic

For Bob and Grace Crockatt

Like gods! we are moulding clay beasts —
nothing as alert as the Scottish Farmer clipped
champions with 'ten to two' ears — the more
I worry at it, the worse mine gets; I have two legs,
forgetting it has to be *four* chips in Grace —
I was looking for *three-D*. She is copying
her porcelain bull, Bob's tomato-stained fingers
pinch his close to hippo. The cocktail sticks
she looked out to make crest hairs are irrelevant,
we finish with Cotoneaster eyes. What conclusions
are we to draw? Our great, stunted embryos are fixed,
as if on islands and uncombed; our pooled,
spare clay is a feeding trough; Bob is in storytelling
heaven and tomorrow will be Pentecost.

Rawburn Transformer

His after-image is as colourful as he is black;
is as stubborn as a Barnett Newman zip;
is a shot weathercock set West; is the actual size
of Mohammed Ali's bandaged fist;
has Estimated Breed Values like barrage balloons;
would take a tonne of antitoxin-worth
of bacteria to fell him; has a heart branded
on his hide; is spring-moulting happily;
is neither solid nor fluid; is energy gestated
into form in a void; will drool, like a Picasso bull
if you stroke him; is a set of questions —
who said that drawing was near to hospitality;
that painting could be a type of prayer;
that Apollo's torso could change you?

Arc

We're saying that man breeds Aberdeen-Angus
because of the relative lengths of their generation
times — otherwise it might as well be the cattle
moulding those men and their wives.
And just as every person is a point at which
the world's appearances cross each-other
gathering, in carousel, like this, so it is
with every animal — and the shape
of this uniqueness, those cattle being horn-less,
must be a halo round their shadow, like a glory,
or like that silver sleeper earring that I find
from time to time and there now, fallen
on the pavement and I know that it's not the same
one and that it will never happen again.

Crisis
22nd March 2001

My father, Bertie, had a set of stories
of animals he'd accidentally run over
with the bread van — the odd pheasant
that hung for while in the garage, a collie
that, as it happens, had been worrying sheep.
Speaking of which, *Today is the tomorrow,
you worried about yesterday,* was a wavy-edged
plaque in our hall, there were cartoon wrinkles
on a man's forehead and a jaunty script,
considering how his anxieties had woken him.
That last week, his great heart fretted about
the foot-and-mouth. As it happens, the brigadier
who marched to Cumbria, with a crisis
on his hands, shared my father's name.

Birtie

I went to visit him, he had bantam hens
and a garden. He'd taught his children to fish
in rivers with their feet, instead of hooks.
He poured me orange juice, he scattered crumbs
on the lawn for his half-blind lab, he said,
to keep her mind alert. *We humans, are nothing
but faeces, fears and vanity, held in a bag of skin.*
But he could talk about art: he defined it
as if it were the plans he'd drawn
for the 24 hour slaughter/48 hour ring cull
at Great Orton – two feedback loops in biro
on his silk cut packet, which in the event
caved in the middle bit – into a fank,
a holding pen, for brigadiers, viruses, windmills.

Doublings

He wanted loyalty, the chanter had been his first love
but his children wouldn't learn the bagpipes
and his Blair Memorial Flute Band neighbours
stole his orange lilies, every eleventh.
Now that the Skye Boat Song has been decoded
for me into Scottish birls and taorluaths,
I am reminded of his two paying pupils,
the grease marks my mother said their jackets
made weekly against the wall by the kitchen table –
fingers in a cluster, mouthpieces hard bit –
one not having practised, one clearly not able
nor musical: a parable. We made ourselves scarce.
These days I am in danger of being exactly
one or the other or of running out of breath.

Memorial

Whose bright idea was to put together
a memorial band for the two Blair brothers
who went under at the Lovers' Retreat (where we saw
the salmon leap) trying to save the Birney girl?
She got sedate accordions, frilled blouses.
Nor do I know how the little couple felt
each year, being swept down Queen's Parade
by the utter swagger of louts with flutes
and cock-a-hoop drums, with my father's orange lilies
shuddering in the strings. Nor do I know
how the leader managed to catch the staff he hurled
towards heaven, blinking back the sun,
but I can guess the name of the tune they played —
brash stuff, glorious, a complete disgrace.

Laird

When our cousins shouldered him that March,
down the road that suddenly seemed all his —
between the painted kerb-stones
and the flags tattering above us —
towards the parked cars and the field;
there were no bagpipes or flutes,
no tuning-up or adjusting drones in the garage,
no women pinning plaids with brooches —
but irises and tulips and Catholic bread-men
enough to feed five thousand and more besides;
we held ourselves tall — his matching twins —
the way we'd been taught for the twelfth
to hold the banner strings; I hummed
Kilmarnock, used for psalms.

Apprentices

I smiled at the last flutter of confetti
when I lifted his Hardie pipes from their box,
to restore them with wads of Silvo,
linseed oil, beeswax; I sliced through twine
that smelt of old spare room, replaced that treacle-
crystalled, animal-skin that used to slime.
Now we have rigged our drones and tied our stocks,
we're a fairy ring of pipers on his lawn,
from as far a-field as Dundee and Nanchang;
our teachers are making encouraging eyebrows
as we stutter through Hot Punch, elbowing
our Gore-Tex bags with zips, pretending
we see Mull across the Minch, for our fathers,
mothers, sisters and anyone who knows us.

Canntaireachd

You would sound a retreat, not because
you'd lost, but to mark with a lilt the end
of the day: *what has been done, has been done;*
what has not, has not; let it rest. Small music
those reels, strathspeys, seven/eights.
You know that idiosyncratic way he had
of — definitely not la-la-ing — his pipe tunes?
Well, for the *piobaireachd*, it seems, there's a whole,
early language of chanting vocables,
so you can memorise those leaping grace-notes
and embellishments. Only a chance remains
that the Gaelic title might be misunderstood:
not *A'bheil thu bronach* 'Are you sad?' rather
Bhraonach, 'fair, as it leaves the honeycomb'.

Yvonne Says You Can Pose Any Question To The Universe

Is my father listening? Oh, every time:
look — when you went to warm up
for the Scotland the Brave set
at the city chambers, before graduation,
in front of all those portraits
of emerald-chained past-provosts;
that rabbit dropping that hopped
from your bagpipes-case, that came
from all your practicing at the allotment,
where your mother pottered
and reminisced about the twelfth,
remember how it merrily bounced
across the plush carpet:
that was his lucky mascot.

IV

The Method I take to do this, is not yet very usual; for instead of using only comparative and superlative Words and intellectual Arguments, I have taken the course to express myself in Terms of Number, Weight, or Measure...and to consider only such Causes, as have visible Foundation in Nature.

- John Locke, 1668

*But thou hast arranged all things by measure
and number and weight....
Because the whole world before thee is like
a speck that tips the scales,
and like a drop of morning dew that falls upon the ground.*

- The Wisdom of Solomon

That The Attitude Influences The Result

Enter: the new research assistant
and he earned twice as much as we did.

His thumbs, we noticed, flexed ninety degrees
at the first joint, he handled the forceps

and decanted the resin in complete patience.
His windscreen-clear sections never puckered

off the knife into the trough. Rather, ultra-thin,
they indented the water like pond-skaters.

It was as if the cells grew on his behalf,
uncontaminated, so that he could embalm

their quiet, stable lives, as clever as turquoise.
Some of us dreaded tilting our flasks. Our instincts

were always right. Black specks, flocking,
seeded from day one: promiscuous, like thrips.

Travels Of Saint Thomas

1.   In the Cave of the Trough

They counteract, do they not?
those pretensions that human truths
are only shadow: here, two dozen thousand
tally-marks of mane and horn and dewlap,
crayoned, poised and warm; and there:
a seal gouged in the belly of a fish:
a veritable zodiac, allowed to feed around
this trough, with us — who stink of paraffin,
the only pair that waft and flicker —
mentally sluggish and bodily swallowed.

2.   In the Tomb of the Eagles

If the hands that shaped these stones into tools
or *your turn to speak* conch pieces, can touch us,
somewhat gleefully, as we grasp for uses,
then the evidence of a chambered cairn is not enough;

but, if when you hauled yourself to stoop underground,
with your eyes and palms wanting, the very walls
gathered, to clasp you at the shoulders, that
would indicate the wingspan of the man.

3.   *In the Snowstorm*

He thought of that Korean girl,
who was choreographed
into the limelight, mouthing ash,
when he saw the schoolboy faltering

to catch snow on his tongue;
and he thought of her supple forgiveness,
when the wagtail pucked orange peel
in gullies between wettening cobbles,

all harlequined, wolf-brave.
But the bow of those lips had delivered
his single word, melting on him
soon and this was a prosperous town
and he was ashamed.

4.   *Tacit*

By convention there is sweet,
Bitter, hot, cold, colour,
But in reality, only ever atoms and void.

Though colours bleed galleries of evidence,
men are rich with return-talk,
and the wind blows a roll-call in the desert.

Comparison Of A Black Labrador With A Sikka Deer Skull

Nose to nose —
indeed, they both seem almost all nose —
those quill curl passageways
wondering back to a plump brain-place;

I shuggled the deer skull
by its sugar-cone tines and he startled
as if those slack teeth could still function.

That week I walked the dog, I thought
he is like the nightmare baby in the attic
that you have forgotten to feed

but he forgives you
in a clumsy pirouette of himself
when you fetch his lead

he has no problem in being too literal,
literal is all he is
meandering the line between skull plates
carrying a ridiculous stick home in his mouth.

Sonnet Of The Noctuoid Moth

*After 'Auditory encoding during the last moment of a moth's life'**

I have been granted 3 conditions,
all referring to the predatory bat:
no-bat,   far-bat,
near-bat. I have been given ears
to listen, to hear the no-bat, far-bat,
near-bat. Each ear has two cells,
and possibly a third, vestigial one.
I am allowed what they are calling
anti-bat manoeuvres — auditory moments —
      evasive flight —
before my death. In real life,
before my death, the situation
may be more erratic, beautifully
      pointless

* Fullard, J. et. al. 2003. *Journal of Experimental Biology*, 206: 281-294

The Herd Sorts Pine-Cones
For Robert Jaffray

He orchestrates his hirsel events
with pine-cone sheep —
little discrete, plump, sibling-things,
which he has collected.

Humming to himself, he arranges them in hefts,
depending on the lie of the land.
He remembers to shoo hungry ewes
from the stack of good hay,

to drift them back to the fold for handling —
he kens them, as his father does.
In daylight, he will lift them, almost perishing,
to scrape for heather shoots in frost.

He brings out and trades his best tups,
cannily, with his friends, swaps yarns,
scolds fluke-worm, sees that the lambs
are well nursed, so his hills will drop fatness.

Valentine
For Bill Ritchie

A moon-drop on the end of a pipette,
a particle of salt, a sheep's egg.
Specifically, he chose her
because she gleamed, radiant.

She must have been winking,
even then, *what's keeping you?*
She also proved to be inquisitive,
a bit of a madam for food, but shy at times.

His skills were in anaesthetics,
electrics, optics, but she possessed
his reason with hope, as fine
as flyaway silk, and teased through fire.

Sheep creep on hillsides
only from a distance,
only held at arms' length = otherwise,
they butt and nibble.

For his photos, he coloured the backdrop
cerulean, as if she were a planet.
On his posters, her cross-section sang,
an open vowel. Should Dolly give Bill

a love song, live solo that she was?
If the soul is skin or where we touch
then, yes, his lungs held her breath
as much as they held his own.

Wordpigs
For Francoise Wemelsfelder

Words are like whole pigs.

What pigs do with their bodies

> is language
> bringing what is inside
> outside
>
> an active thing
> like dancing;

a pig is a whole animal, doing language.

Familiar —
cornea valve gooseflesh belly breast
pale iris
backs as vulnerable
as those of little toads or babies

> prone at times to wasting disease
>
> breathing in heaves we recognise
>
> that we have shared before —
>
> a blue liquid overdose comes as a kindness
>
> a butterfly of blood is left on the ear;

pigs are whole animals

>   gregarious
>   hierarchical
>   segregated

farrowing in pens
in case the young are crushed
weaned
and stalled in age-groups
arranged on a flat page finishing house

if you visit

>   the words will rustle
>   through bedding straw
>   will flock to flatter you
>   with wet disc noses
>   biting, sore at your wellingtons
>   perhaps because they are bored;

perhaps they would be happier in mud

feeling for knowledge

>   and feeling is a thing you do
>   like rooting
>   like dancing

Man and Atoms

A man's job is to compose,
so he will see the world
first as little atoms,
his first beginnings.

He will even refer to them
as 'first beginnings',
when he explains that, in themselves,
these primordial units
have no colour, no scent.

Don't take this the wrong way,
he encourages any of us
who are curious,
they are not little animalcules
with guts or laughter,
nor do they shimmer
like goldfish in sunlight,

nor do they think
but, from time to time,
they do swerve.
And in doing so, he muses,
they coax from doubt new houses,
peopled with little twin-gods,
the things the heart allows.

Suddenly, the man
has been introduced
to all that has already happened
and sees that time is amorphous, draped
on the surface of things.
At last, he knows that he is loved.
And afraid is how he feels.

Number, Weight And Measure

he will just have muttered,
as the glass-walled lift
stalls, midway between floors.
My mother and Francis Bacon — trapped!
Oh there'll be a startled reaction
but they'll get on fine, my mother
will straighten his ruffle
and offer to hem with whipstitch
the unravelled section.

He will give in to the boredom
and borrow a felt pen, with interest,
to join freckles on the back of her hand —
Auriga, Cassiopeia, he'll make.
He will ask about the surroundings,
she won't know from that distance —
on the cusp of the fourth floor up —
crouching to peer out, that 'beautiful'
is spelt bizarrely on the concrete cycle-path;

he won't know that celestial harmonies
have now gone metric nor that she is left-handed,
but they'll get on; in common, in past lives,
they have steered nature's malevolence to a halt —
she with cloths draped over mirrors
in a thunderstorm, he with measured
curves as normal as magnolia.
Oh, neither are superstitious (shudder
from the lift), they share a saviour.

Cleave
Schistosoma mansoni

If all can be pared
to the one essence,
this dual creature
contrives best:
Schist

because
the female body
splits the male
they lie,
in copula, for years,

shedding only eggs
as tears.
It would be
without meaning
to put words

urgent or *enjoyment*
in the mouth
of the *Schistosome,*
since the mouth
is mouthing no mouth.

In the constant
bearing
of your pain
I feel
that I am healed.

Hybrid

We were always drawing: horses, ballerinas
but I remember once making a felt pen outline
of a blade of grass, so that it bent in the middle
as if in a strong wind — not Northern Irish grass,
which doesn't as I recall, grow in rigid, broad blades,
but rather soft or thin clumps, nor the green
rushes which we squashed when we cleverly hopped from
one to another, to avoid sinking in the bog,

a rush stem wouldn't bend but it would spring
or break to show the white inside the cylinder.
No, the blade I drew was the sort you'd get fanned out
as part of a palm, and the wind had switched it
to horizontal, half-way down its length. I remember the occasion
of this throw-away sketch because my mother
was quite blown away by the effect, which I'd copied
from a comic, I suppose, a cartoon frond of grass.

But when I was much younger, again it must have been
my mother who'd left a religious comic sitting around,
a tract aimed at teenagers, and I caught sight
of a half-man half-dog, it's very detailed ring-collar
and the long, side-view dog's snout with teeth
were appalling, I never copied it on any page
but into my parents' wardrobe and under the bed.
I was very young, I had no inkling of Egyptian gods,

this was a hybrid creature that invoked a hybrid fear
that stayed with me for a decade and more —
a tall thin horror with a cold man's legs
and a broad gold torque and a dog's jaw,
and all worshipped with palms.
Did it bother me because I knew we are not animals?
Or, if we are, we are of one whole type, not jumbled
and certainly not a composite of just two species.

If *to imagine* separates us from the animals,
we get this wrong at times, we provoke our own fears.
They used to harvest leeches by sending lads
to wade in the river and the leeches would latch onto
their boots, imagining they were horses.
Not symbolic horses, not apocalyptic horses
nor really even mistakenly horses, but simply
blood sources other than themselves, happily,

which on that day differed. Because we have been taught,
we too are as fleeting as a blade of grass,
it may be the food or the symbol — milk or blood
or excrement or bread — that attracts us forward
on that day which is different.
It may be the chance to connect. When you asked
about reincarnation I blurted: a dog — on a windswept plain
where there were palms waving and a wide river.

Second Wind
For Miriam

In the way that god's spirit
might as well be she,
who winnows life, why not?
So, why not, a Weimeraner
at evening prayer?
That will have been
the provost's logic
besides, it was her last service,
and maybe, she was musing:
if it's a choice
between the truth
and the legend, she'd take
the legend every time.
All right for her,
Robert was the warrior
who kept the vanilla-brute
with her forget-me-not eyes
under wraps, till the winding up —
the Lord Dismiss Us
— and she's off! A race horse
at the starting gates,
a Solomon forsaking wisdom,
a king, after interregnum.
Had the minutes been sentient,
they'd have muttered
such behaviour!
as she legged it

down the badly ruptured,
chequered aisle.
Twice married, ex-nun
the papers would have put
the preface,
had they been there.
But I'm willing to bet
the seconds were vigilant,
squiggling, even, to witness
the courting from square
to square, urging,
Hola allelujah!
as they echo on a Sunday,
in the windswept village
she retired to,
where the breath of god
is not a stutter, but *legato;*
where the bulk of things
has yet to be restored.

Key

Trust a poet to invent
an anti-rainbow, colour active
at the knife edge of the prism
where light meets dark meets light
to call the soul's night
peach blossom.

Think of the tired river
in your weary home town
slipping along dank pubs,
and commercial premises
suddenly yelling Himalayan balsam:
that shade.

Or the railway lines' rose-bay willowherb.
Incorrigible. A mathematical man promised
once: when my numbers come in
I'll buy you a barge.
You see it as much as you know him
to be gone —

painted with dragonflies,
bonnie blue ribbons, throwing milky shadows.
But there are weeds for widows
somewhere speared
between the benweed
and the Johnston's blue;

between the very castanets you brandished,
soft burrs spurring morning.

Galatea

You, with your talk
sculpted Galatea —
so convincingly
she would even have thought
of herself as marble.

One word here, one here;
you refined her silence,
expected her beauty —
she lay and her body
curved this way.

At last she felt
an arrow like ice
not as it pierced
but its arrival.
She woke. She spoke the shape
you listening made her.

Garden

So there is a waiting in darkness
where scraps of *broderie anglaise*
have become windswept
and there is a snail sleeping, behind glass
on the plastic face of the Divine.

But his blind place
is my peaceful one;
his hell is where the hills grow fennel
and figs are ready to rain.

The first cockcrow screams
as if every solid fact
were taking flight.
The white fork
will be too beautiful for us to describe.

As faith is to mountains,
so is a fleeting thought to truth.
The only constant is the pace of light.
The only thing that's left to do now, is to meet.